American Bison

by Grace Hansen

Abdo
ANIMALS OF
NORTH AMERICA
Kids

abdopublishing.com

Published by Abdo Kids, a division of ABDO, PO Box 398166, Minneapolis, Minnesota 55439.

Copyright © 2016 by Abdo Consulting Group, Inc. International copyrights reserved in all countries. No part of this book may be reproduced in any form without written permission from the publisher.

Printed in the United States of America, North Mankato, Minnesota.

102015

012016

 THIS BOOK CONTAINS RECYCLED MATERIALS

Photo Credits: iStock, Shutterstock

Production Contributors: Teddy Borth, Jennie Forsberg, Grace Hansen

Design Contributors: Laura Mitchell, Dorothy Toth

Library of Congress Control Number: 2015941757

Cataloging-in-Publication Data

Hansen, Grace.

 American bison / Grace Hansen.

  p. cm. -- (Animals of North America)

ISBN 978-1-68080-107-1 (lib. bdg.)

Includes index.

1. American bison--Juvenile literature. 2. Bison--Juvenile literature.   I. Title.

599.64/3--dc23

            2015941757

Table of Contents

American Bison

American bison live on the Great Plains. The Great Plains are in the United States and Canada. Bison live in Alaska, too.

4

5

Bison are very big. They are the heaviest land animals in North America.

Bison have strong legs.

They have large **hooves**.

Bison have long brown hair. The hair is very thick. It keeps them warm in winter. Bison **shed** in spring.

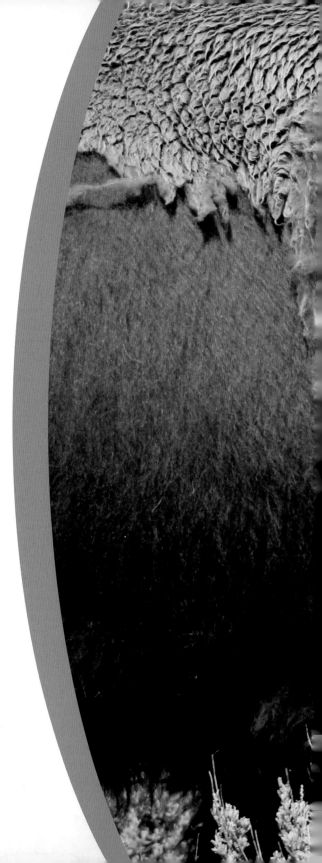

Bison have two horns on the tops of their heads. The horns are short and curved. **Bulls** use their horns to fight.

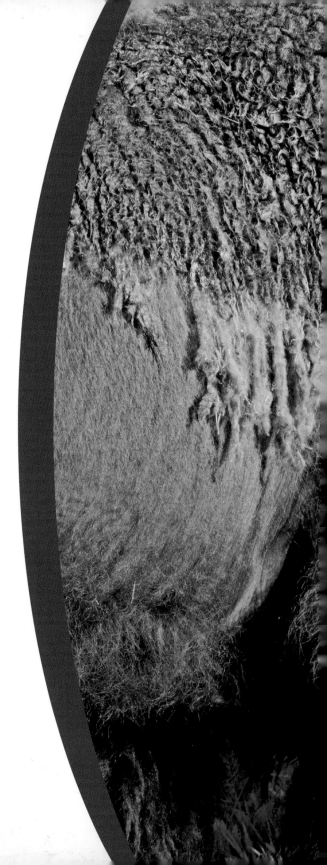

13

A bison has a large hump on its back. The hump is strong. It **supports** the large head.

15

Grazing & Food

Bison are grazers.

They eat all day long.

Bison eat most plants that grow in grasslands. They eat grasses and shrubs. They also eat twigs.

19

Baby Bison

Baby bison are called calves. Calves have reddish hair. Mothers nurse their calves for 6 months.

More Facts

- A group of bison living together is called a band.

- Bison use their humps to swing their heads back and forth. This helps them move snow in winter. There is grass to eat under the snow!

- Female bison weigh up to 1,200 pounds (544 kg). Males can weigh 2,000 pounds (907 kg)!

Glossary

bull – a male bison.

grazer – an animal that continuously feeds on vegetation.

hooves – the hard, protective coverings on the feet of some animals.

shed – hair falling off naturally.

support – to hold up.

Index

abdokids.com

Use this code to log on to abdokids.com and access crafts, games, videos, and more!

Abdo Kids Code:
AAK1071